Help! How Do I Pray?

A JESUS-CENTERED GUIDE J.

HELP! HOW DO I PRAY?

Lifetree™ is an imprint of Group Publishing, Inc.

Visit our website: group.com

Written by Mikal Keefer

Library of Congress Cataloging-in-Publication Data

Names: Group Publishing.
Title: Help! How Do I Pray?
Description: First American paperback [edition]. | Loveland, Colorado : Group Publishing, Inc., 2018. | Series: A Jesus-centered guide
Identifiers: LCCN 2017052348 | ISBN 9781470753207 (pbk.)
Subjects: LCSH: Prayer--Christianity.
Classification: LCC BV215 .H475 2018 | DDC 248.3/2--dc23 LC record available at https://lccn.loc.gov/2017052348

ISBN: 978-1-4707-5320-7 (softcover)

ISBN: 978-1-4707-5321-4 (ePub)

Printed in the United States of America.

10 9 8 7 6 5 4 3 2 1 27 26 25 24 23 22 21 20 19 18

TABLE OF CONTENTS

"Rejoice in our confident hope. Be patient in trouble, and keep on praying."
Romans 12:12

INTRODUCTION

Everyone tells you that you *should* pray.

And you *want* to pray.

Really, you do.

But while others blissfully recount how "Jesus told me..." or "God soothed my soul when..." you mostly have this to report: "I fell asleep."

So what's the story? Is everyone else lying...or is there a secret about prayer that you don't know? Something that would help you have a prayer life that actually has a pulse?

We talked with people who have meaningful, authentic prayer lives and summarized their advice for you here in this handy little guide to prayer.

Some of it you've heard before—but never quite like this. And some of what our friends have shared will surprise you...in a good way.

Just do this for us—and for yourself as well: Be willing.

Be willing to rethink what prayer is and how it fits into your life.

Be willing to experiment a bit.

And be willing to be honest—because whatever else prayer is, it *must* be honest. Prayer is a place to meet Jesus…but it's a place where there's no room for hiding.

Though it *is* a place with ample room to talk, laugh, and play.

So get ready to actually *enjoy* prayer and to experience it in a way you've not experienced it before.

WHAT IS PRAYER, ANYWAY?

Imagine for a moment you've stepped through the looking glass into a perfect garden oasis.

Fragrant blossoms and fruit trees perfume the air. A cool evening breeze whispers through leaves and tall grass as, above, a slowly sinking sun paints delicate clouds a thousand shades of gold.

Your senses are overwhelmed as you turn slowly in a circle, taking it all in. You've simply never been anywhere this beautiful, never imagined anywhere could *be* this beautiful.

And then you see them, stepping out from behind a cascade of tall flowers—a man, a woman, and, walking between them, the God of the universe.

They're talking as they walk, those three. About the day, the garden, one another. The bright sparkle of Eve's laughter floats across the garden, and God's voice soothes all who hear it—every plant, insect, and animal resting nearby.

It's a conversation between friends.

A conversation—and a prayer.

No heads are bowed, no eyes are closed (good thing, too—Adam's naked, and that's a rosebush in front of him), and all three are laughing loud and long.

But this is as pure a prayer as you'll find anywhere in the Bible.

God and his creation in joyful, relaxed intimacy—prayer doesn't get any better. Not for Adam and Eve, and not for you.

God's built you for exactly that sort of intimacy with him. He's built you to be his friend. For the two of you to talk, listen, and share the occasional playful nudge in the ribs. To do what friends do.

If that's what you're hungry for—loving, satisfying, joyful conversations with God—*great.* You and God are on the same page.

But what will it take for you to enjoy a walk in the garden with God? To have that sort of intimacy? For prayer to be more than a duty? For you to be able to relax into a natural conversation rather than default to formulas?

It starts with a simple truth: *Prayer is all about relationship.*

Period.

It's not really about how well you talk or even what you talk about. It's who else is in the conversation. That's the most important thing.

If there's a common theme running through the helpful tips about prayer you'll find in this guide, it's this: *Focus on your relationship with God.*

That's what puts you in the garden and keeps you there. That's what brushes the dust off prayer and breathes fresh life into your time with God.

Though there's also this: We can easily get in our own way when it comes to prayer. So let's begin by clearing away a bit of brush that might be crowding the path you want to walk with God.

Let's deal with a few weeds that can choke out your fruitful prayer life.

WEED 1: There's No Point in Praying

If God already knows everything, why bother filing a report? He knows what you need and what's up in your life; he can decide what—if anything—he wants to do about it.

Um…remember how prayer is all about relationship?

That's why God wants the communication with you—because of your friendship. True, you probably won't say or do anything that surprises God, but he's interested in your take on things. You're in this relationship together, and God gives you a tremendous amount of respect as you navigate life.

Look, intimacy is scary. That's one reason there's so little of it.

And intimacy with God is scary, too, at least at first. What will he do if you tell him what's really going on? What's actually bubbling beneath the surface?

What if God knew what you were *really* thinking?

Spoiler alert: He does know...and he loves you anyway. He not only loves you, he *likes* you—and calls you his friend. Now and then, when you're praying, God slides a glance over at an angel, nods your direction, and says, "That one? That's some of my best work right there."

And *that's* the point of praying: To delight God. To deepen your friendship with him. And to invite him to speak into your life.

Because that's what friends do.

WEED 2: Prayer Is Boring

Can't argue with you there: Reciting words at the ceiling is about as boring as boring gets.

But having a conversation with God? One in which you're both talking about what's most important to you? That's anything *but* boring—and exactly where you're headed.

So no matter what your past experiences with prayer have been, please be willing to engage in prayer again—minus the baggage you usually haul along with you when you pray.

Set aside all the "shoulds" that attach to prayer like barnacles clinging to a boat. Scrape off the expectations about how you should pray, when you should pray, and why you should pray.

Toss all the formulas and recipes overboard and be willing to consider prayer from a new point of view—one that's all about a friendship with God. One that centers on Jesus.

And while you're busy scrubbing your prayer deck clean, deep-six any shame and guilt you feel about how your prayer life has looked in the past. There's nothing beneficial about guilting yourself into having a conversation with God.

And it's hard to picture God getting all excited and tingly about receiving a distracted, obligatory call.

Prayer boring? Not the way *you'll* be praying.

WEED 3: Prayer Doesn't Work

Depending on what you expect prayer to accomplish, you're right.

But you're also wrong.

Prayer was never intended to be measured by how many requests you were granted after you ran your list by God. Or by how many miracles were delivered when only God's intervention could fix what was broken.

Prayer is a relationship...a friendship with God.

If you and God are communicating, prayer is working.

We'll dive deeper into what it means for prayer to "work," but for now let's consider who's on the other end of the line when you pray.

DECIDE WHO YOU'RE TALKING TO

Two Baylor University sociologists, Paul Froese and Christopher Bader, decided to find out how Americans view God.

What they uncovered through their surveys may shed a great deal of light on how and why you do—or don't—pray.

In their book, *America's Four Gods: What We Say About God—And What That Says About Us,* Froese and Bader report Americans have four basic concepts of God:

The authoritative God is one who's actively engaged in history and taking careful notes about who is and isn't following him. This version of God is very willing to administer harsh punishment to those who don't fall in line. About 28 percent of survey respondents painted this picture when explaining how they view God.

Then there's the distant God. This is God as a cosmic force who set the universe spinning but has zero concern about the individuals in it or the details of their daily lives. About 24 percent of Americans see God this way.

The benevolent God is engaged in the world and loves and supports people as they care for others. He's a comforter and a powerful force for good. Twenty-two percent of survey respondents described God in this way.

Another 21 percent portrayed God as a critical God, a God who keeps an eye on what's happening in this world but is putting off settling accounts until the next world. He's mostly keeping tabs on injustices so he can right them when the right time comes.

It's likely your view of God is summed up in one of those four sketches of God—as authoritative, distant, benevolent, or critical.

And understanding your view matters—because if prayer is communication, it makes sense to know who you're communicating with.

So let's pause and give you a chance to do a little self-discovery.

Grab a pencil or pen...you're about to take a pop quiz.

All set?

Now turn to page 16 where you'll see those four descriptions of God in four corners of a box. Your job is to circle the description that best describes God as you were raised to view him.

So think back: When you were a child, how was God explained to you? As a straighten-up-or-else authoritarian? As a distant or absent force who may exist but doesn't care about you?

Or maybe you viewed God as benevolent—always aware of you, always loving, always willing to engage with you.

Or maybe you saw God as critical. He was there, but he was more of a cosmic accountant who will even up the score in heaven. He wasn't all that concerned about getting mixed up with you here on earth.

Circle one of the four descriptions, and then, in the box, jot down how that view of God was shaped in you. Maybe it was shaped by what your parents said or did, or perhaps you attended a Sunday school of some sort that shaped your perception of God.

However you were introduced to God, describe it in the box.

HOW I VIEWED GOD AS I WAS GROWING UP

AUTHORITATIVE

DISTANT

BENEVOLENT

CRITICAL

Now let's talk about how you view God today.

Maybe it's the same way you saw him when you were a child. Or perhaps your view has shifted to another corner.

In the box on page 18, please circle the description of God that best reflects how you view God *now.*

If you've shifted corners, what prompted you to change your view of God? What—or who—influenced your thinking? Write about that in the box.

Please don't skip over this opportunity to explore how you've viewed God in the past and how you view him today. These few pages are the most important in this little book because they get at the very heart of your relationship—or lack of relationship—with God.

HOW I VIEW GOD TODAY

AUTHORITATIVE

DISTANT

BENEVOLENT

CRITICAL

Now pause for a moment to consider what you circled...and what you wrote.

If you view God as authoritative, it makes perfect sense to spend as little time with him as possible. Doing anything else would be like befriending the vice principal of discipline back when you were in middle school; the better she got to know you, the more detention was heading your way.

Better to just keep quiet and hope to fly under the radar.

There's no relaxed intimacy to be had with an authoritative God; it makes perfect sense for you to be on your guard around him...and to be around him as little as possible.

And praying to a distant God? What's the point? It's not as if he's paying attention or cares what you say. You might as well be whispering into a pillow and hoping someone a thousand miles away hears you.

A critical God might make a note about what you pray, but he won't get involved in details or intervene on your behalf.

But if you view God as benevolent—someone who has your best interests at heart, who wants to hang out with you, and who's as welcoming as he is loving—now *that's* someone you might want to spend time with.

If that's how you view God, then prayer makes sense as something other than a spiritual exercise or a discipline intended to placate God.

And a benevolent God is exactly who Jesus described when he described God. It's exactly what he modeled through his own actions. A benevolent God who stands on the porch scanning the horizon, waiting for a prodigal son to return. A benevolent God who's so hungry for relationship and reconciliation that he comes to earth in the person of Jesus to die for you.

Does that mean God has no authority, that he's a soft teddy bear who radiates only love?

God *certainly* has authority—but he uses it in a loving, redemptive way.

First and foremost, God is love. He's benevolent.

“

But anyone
who does not love
does not know God,
for God is love.

”

1 John 4:8

If our researcher friends are right, the odds are you circled something other than *benevolent* in your two boxes. Perhaps this is because of how you were raised, or because that's how God has been described to you in sermon after sermon, or because of an event in your life when God seemed far more concerned about judging you than riding to your rescue.

But if Jesus is right when he describes God as good and loving—and if you want a prayer life that goes beyond duty to discovery and friendship—you need to find your way to the benevolent corner.

God will meet you wherever you are, but joy in prayer comes when you relate to God as a friend rather than as a taskmaster.

So a request: Would you be willing to give God the benefit of the doubt? To treat him as if he's both benevolent and interested in your life to see whether he comes through for you?

You've nothing to lose...and a universe of friendship to gain.

David wrote this in Psalm 34:8: "Taste and see that the Lord is good. Oh, the joys of those who take refuge in him!"

Put David's words to the test: Give God a chance to show you who he *really* is.

PAUSE TO PONDER

While you have a pen handy, write a quick note to God on page 24. Tell God how you view him—and why. And tell him what it would take for you to trust that he's truly benevolent, truly caring, and truly engaged in your life. Even if you circled the word *benevolent,* write a note. Trust grows; tell God what it will take to deepen your trust in him.

It's okay to be honest. Nothing you write will surprise him. And if he's really benevolent, he'll welcome your transparency.

Dear God,

Sincerely,

IF TALKING WITH SOMEONE YOU CAN'T SEE FEELS WEIRD...

If you find it hard to focus on someone you can't see, you're not alone. People throughout history have struggled with that peculiarity about prayer—though few of them have had as much practice as you've had.

Think about it: You talk with people you can't see all the time.

You pull out your cellphone and make a call. You text on a tablet. You email from a laptop. Depending on your age, more than half of your communication may be with people who aren't physically with you.

The difference is this: You're absolutely certain the person on the other end of your technological communication is actually there. You *know* the person is real.

When you're dealing with God, you take it on faith…and that's sometimes a challenge.

Plus, when you're unsure God's answering, it's easy to let your focus fade. To start talking on autopilot. To drift and keep drifting.

So, two issues to resolve if you're to have a more satisfying prayer life: First, have confidence that you're part of a conversation rather than just talking to yourself. And second, keep your focus sharp as you talk with a God you can't see.

That first challenge is all about your relationship with God. As you and God spend more time together, as you come to know his voice, your confidence in his presence will grow.

And the second challenge is one you can do something about right now.

Following are three prayer experiments for you to try. You may discover that one or more of them may energize your ability to speak with God in spite of his lack of visibility. Or some of them may be complete flops.

Either way, it's okay. These experiments are just that: experiments, not prescriptions. Give each one a try, and then jot a few notes about how it felt. You can repeat or abandon as you see fit.

Or better yet, your experiments may spark an idea—which could be coming from God, by the way (just sayin')—that will unlock a way to a more intimate prayer life with the God who's there, visible or not.

EXPERIMENT 1: The Prayer Chair

Pull two chairs into position for a comfortable conversation. Sit in one and imagine Jesus sitting in the other.

Picture Jesus the way he probably looked—a Jewish guy with a wide smile. Dark, weathered skin. Hands thick with calluses from his work as a carpenter. Dusty feet from a long walk that brought him to you.

Imagine his face—it's open, inviting. He's comfortable in his own skin and happy to see you. He's got a twinkle in his eye; he's been looking forward to this conversation.

His eyes are quick and understanding. And he's leaning forward, ready to hear and be heard.

Got all that in mind?

Now...pray.

Eyes wide open, imagination fully engaged, have a conversation with the Jesus who's sitting across from you. And make it a conversation, not a monologue. Pause often. Be willing to hear what he says.

Listen for a word…or for an image to come to mind…or even a snatch of a song or a Bible verse. But keep your focus on the chair and the man in it.

If you feel your focus beginning to fade, just wrap up. You can always invite Jesus for more conversation later. He's amazingly willing to reschedule.

When you've finished, make a few notes below. How did it go, and are you willing to do this again?

EXPERIMENT 2: Call God

Whatever phone you normally use to connect with friends, pull it out, kill the sound so you won't be interrupted, and put it to your ear.

Now pray.

If you normally pace around as you talk on the phone, give yourself permission to do the same with this call. If you often doodle, get to doodling.

Remember to ask Jesus what he has in mind for you before ringing off. And pay attention—you'd be surprised what a talker Jesus can be if someone's listening.

Clearly you won't be punching in a number but… well, you *could.* If you have a close friend whose account is set up to accept long voice messages, you can leave a message at that number. It'll be a wrong number your friend isn't likely to forget.

When you've finished, make a few notes below. How did it go, and are you willing to do this again?

EXPERIMENT 3: Write to God

Send God an email or text. Or a letter. However you write to your other friends, use that approach to write to God.

The trick is to be in the moment. This is more a letter home from camp than a formal address to the nations. Hurry through your letter, unconcerned with spelling and penmanship. Move along as quickly as possible.

Pour it out...and then read it aloud (maybe you *should* have paid a bit of attention to your penmanship!) and listen to what you've said. When you ask a question or make an assumption or statement, pause to listen.

What, if anything, do you hear?

Stretch that attention out over the next day or two. Sometimes God answers—but quietly and in his own time.

When you've finished, make a few notes below. How did it go, and are you willing to do this again?

“

Are any of you
suffering hardships?
You should pray.
Are any of you happy?
You should sing
praises.

”

James 5:13

IF YOUR PRAYERS AREN'T WORKING...

For most Christians, "not working" means that the situation about which we're praying hasn't improved. There's no observable evidence that God is working.

Your mother's cancer still isn't responding to the chemo treatments.

The job is as miserable today as it was yesterday.

The lottery remains un-won—at least by you.

So doubt sets in: Is it that God isn't answering, or is there something you're doing wrong? Maybe he doesn't love you after all. Or maybe you've gotten the formula mixed up somehow. You're not adding enough worship to the prayer mix, or you've struck the wrong tone with God and offended him somehow.

There's an example of prayer in the Old Testament's book of 1 Kings that perfectly portrays two approaches to prayer…and what happens with each.

In a nutshell: At God's behest, the prophet Elijah goes to see Israel's king, Ahab, who's none too happy with Elijah. A three-year drought has brought disaster to Israel, and, until Israel turns to God, Elijah has no intention of asking God to send rain.

Elijah has a proposal for Ahab: Invite more than 800 prophets of the false gods to meet him on Mount Carmel. They'll take turns praying and then see who answers: Ahab's gods or Elijah's God.

An altar is built, a bull slaughtered, and the prophets of Baal and Asherah go first. They pray with great sincerity—and hear nothing from their gods. So they pray louder. Still nothing. Eventually they're cutting themselves with swords and spears, worshipping their gods with all their might.

And still a resounding nothing in return.

Elijah builds an altar, piles wood on the stones, and then lays pieces of a freshly sacrificed bull on the wood. Douses the entire business with water—three times.

He then asks God to show himself so all those watching will see with certainty that Elijah's God is the true God.

Fire instantly sizzles down from on high, obliterating the sacrifice, the wood, even the stone altar.

Request granted…in a spectacular way.

But as far as prayer logistics go, it's the false prophets who did the better job. They prayed longer, louder, and with far greater intensity. They kept at it even when mocked, even when it appeared that their gods weren't listening. With the possible exception of the self-mutilation, they're the clear winners in doubling down on technique.

Elijah's prayer was brief and not especially elegant. There was nothing fancy or formal. It was as if he was having a conversation, talking with a respected friend.

And God's response was instant and astonishing.

True, the prophets of Baal and Asherah were praying to the wrong gods. And asking for the wrong thing—something clearly outside of God's will. Elijah had an inside edge they couldn't possibly overcome.

And that's the point: The outcome of that Mount Carmel contest was never about how someone prayed. Rather, it was about who else was in the conversation…and what God wanted to accomplish in the situation.

When you aren't getting lightning bolts from heaven in response to your prayers, it's tempting to think God's failing to keep his end of the bargain.

After all, you're asking and asking in the right way: with humility, deference, and the expectation of a response. You've done your part, so it's up to God to make good on his end of the transaction.

But God has never viewed prayer as a transaction. He's looking for transformation instead. And going to him so he can walk with you through your mother's chemo or a work problem or a financial setback is transformational—because you're walking through the situation *with him*.

It changes *you* no matter how the *issue* resolves.

Yes, sometimes God works a miracle of physics or timing to make himself unmistakably known in a situation. But often he doesn't. And he's there either way.

It's unfair to be disappointed if God doesn't meet your demands and relieve your suffering because he never promises to always do either. He's not shorting you if he doesn't pull off a quick fix.

He's *with* you—and acknowledging that is prayer.

Prayer that's working because God has shown up.

PAUSE TO PONDER

Write about a time you felt disappointed in God because your expectations weren't met. What happened? And what did you do with your disappointment?

Share this story with God. He's probably got a few stories to tell you about dealing with disappointment as well. Should make for quite a conversation!

Make an honest list of your expectations about prayer: What do you most often expect will happen when you pray? How do you expect prayer to change you, if at all? your circumstances? God's mind? Why do you have these expectations, and how do you typically react when those expectations aren't met?

Share your list with God. Talk it over. Ask him which items he agrees are fair expectations to carry with you into prayer.

EXPERIMENT 1: Expectation Expression

Maybe this has happened to you: You're with a spouse or friend and slowly notice a certain tight-lipped tension is almost radiating off the other person.

And that's when you realize that something was expected of you and you didn't deliver. And when you ask what that something might be, you hear the dreaded words "Well, if you don't know..."

How frustrating is that? And disrespectful. It's never helpful to expect others to read our minds and meet our unstated expectations.

Yet we often put God in just that spot. We resent God for not responding when we've not taken the time to come to him with a request.

How much better to have an honest conversation. To say, "Because I trust you and our relationship, I want to tell you directly what I'd like you to do for me."

But that's a hard conversation to have. It feels presumptuous, as if you're making demands. And it's an especially hard conversation if the other person in the relationship isn't like anyone else you know. If it's God himself.

So give honest communication a try in a human relationship first. In the next few days, sit down with a spouse or friend, and letting the other person know this is a trial run, ask for two minutes to make clear a request you have of the person. Something like... which side of the driveway to park on. Who's going to set up the next dinner date. How you'd like to split dog-walking duties. Anything that's specific and not going to trigger an argument.

When you've finished, make a few notes below. How did it go...and are you willing to do this again, this time with God? And about far more than dog walking?

IF PRAYING FEELS LIKE A CHORE...

Read a chapter of the Bible...*check*.

Avoid swearing...*check*.

Pay quarterly taxes...*check*.

Pray before every meal and at bedtime...*check*.

If that's where prayer fits in your life—as one more task to check off so you're doing everything you should be doing, no wonder it feels like a chore.

It *is* a chore.

So maybe it's time to pull prayer off your to-do list. Because if that's why you're praying, then you're not talking with God in the context of relationship. Instead, your prayers are prompted by routine, tradition, or guilt.

There's no delight there. No joy. No transformation.

But what if you treated God the way you treat other friends? If you didn't reach out on a rigid schedule but rather when the desire to connect with your friend struck you? Or you heard from your friend and eagerly responded?

In other words, if you treated prayer as less of a "supposed to" and more as a "want to"?

For instance, are you aware that nowhere in the Bible are you commanded to pray before eating a meal? It's a convenient time to be grateful, but anyone who's watched mashed potatoes turn into cement during an overzealous Thanksgiving dinner prayer knows the pain of tradition.

It would have been just as meaningful—perhaps more so—to pause mid-meal and take 60 seconds to thank God for the wonder of the just-right turkey, the savory stuffing, the tangy cranberry sauce.

So let's do a few experiments, shall we?

Let's add some spontaneity and adventure to your prayer life and see what happens.

EXPERIMENT 1: Set an Alarm

Ask someone to set the alarm on your cellphone for a random time between 9 a.m. and 5 p.m. Don't check to see what time was selected.

When the alarm goes off, look around you and ask Jesus what you can pray about in your present situation. If you're with people, perhaps you'll be directed to pray for one of them. If you're mid-task, invite Jesus into whatever you're doing and see how that affects the process and outcome.

Oh, and be sure your friend sets the alarm to the "vibrate only" setting. Otherwise you may have some explaining to do when your phone explodes in the middle of a staff meeting or eye exam.

Once you've given this a try, use the space below to jot a few notes about the experience. How did it go, and are you willing to do this again?

EXPERIMENT 2: Siren Prayer Prompt

A siren rarely means good news. When ambulances, police cars, or fire engines go rushing to a scene, something's happening that could use prayer.

Lower the volume of your car radio (good idea anyway, you rocker, you) so you can keep an ear tuned for the wail of a siren.

When you hear one, ask Jesus what you should pray about.

Then pray.

You may never know the reason a first responder is zooming past you or how the crisis resolves. But does that really matter? You're talking with someone who's already fully informed and has the situation in hand.

Your part is simply to ask how you can pray and then do as you're asked.

Once you've given this a try, jot a few notes about the experience. How did it go, and are you willing to do this again?

EXPERIMENT 3: Emotion Devotion

If you're around people, you're around emotions.

So do this today: Pay close attention to the people around you, and when you detect a negative emotion playing out across the face of someone, pray for that person.

Perhaps a co-worker is stressed. Or a family member is angry. Maybe you can hear sadness in the voice of a friend who calls on the phone, even if she says everything is fine.

Whatever you pick up, invite Jesus into the situation.

You may feel prompted to speak about what you see or hear, to ask if there's anything you can do. Or you may simply pray.

Either way, you're being helpful.

Once you've given this a try, jot a few notes about the experience. How did it go, and are you willing to do this again?

“I am
praying to you
because I know
you will answer,
O God. Bend down
and listen as
I pray.”

Psalm 17:6

IF YOU'RE NOT SURE YOU'VE BEEN GOOD ENOUGH TO PRAY...

Nothing shuts down your enthusiasm for prayer like being afraid that God doesn't consider you worthy of interrupting him, or if you believe you'd best steer clear of God until you straighten up your act.

If that's how you feel, here's some good news, followed by some even better news.

The good news: God already knows you're far from perfect, and he still calls you his friend. So there's no need to hide anything from God—he already knows about everything you've stuffed into the shadows.

And the even better news: You and God are in a friendship, *not* a performance review.

Yes, there are things you can do that will deepen or damage your friendship with God. That's true of all your friendships, and if you value them, you'll choose to do what helps them flourish.

Here's a quick tour of a few things the Bible says will not only strengthen your friendship with God, but also improve your prayer life along the way.

BE TRANSPARENT

In every friendship there's light, breezy stuff that's easy to talk about as well as topics that are less fun to discuss. Your friendship with God deepens if you're willing to lay everything on the table, including those things you'd rather hide, those things that God might be eager to transform in you.

Addictions. Stubborn self-reliance. Cynicism.

Attempting to hide from God limits your relationship with him. You hold him at arm's length, keeping his healing away from those very things in you that need his touch most.

A psalmist wrote this: "If I had not confessed the sin in my heart, the Lord would not have listened" (Psalm 66:18).

Transparency matters in every friendship but especially in your friendship with God. So talk about the important things—all of them.

TRUST GOD

God calls you his friend, and he means it. His desire to be in constant communication with you is heartfelt and sincere.

You have no friend more trustworthy than God, no friend more willing to stick close when the vultures circle and storm clouds gather overhead.

A friend like God is worthy of trust—so trust him. Lean on him. Listen when he speaks, and speak your own mind freely, knowing he's listening.

And ever and always keep the faith. When you do, good things happen.

VALUE YOUR FRIENDSHIP WITH GOD

It's not a relationship to take lightly or to dust off only when there's something you want.

In the same way you'd quickly tire of a buddy who calls only when he wants something, God's looking for more in his friendship with you than simply being a request line. He's remarkably generous, but it matters to God *why* you're in this friendship with him.

James shared this insight about prayer with people who apparently weren't getting what they expected from God: "And even when you ask, you don't get it because your motives are all wrong—you want only what will give you pleasure" (James 4:3).

Your friendship with God is richer and more fulfilling when you come to him for more than help, when you come with a sincere desire to let him mold you into the person he created you to be: one whose prayers reflect a heart given to him.

TREAT OTHERS THE WAY GOD TREATS YOU

Especially when it comes to forgiving others.

There's an especially uncomfortable clause in Jesus' model prayer, one he shared when his disciples asked him to be their prayer coach: "Forgive us our sins, *as we forgive those who sin against us*" (Luke 11:4).

Just guessing, but it's likely that you frequently ask God to forgive you. If that's the case, Jesus apparently expects you to forgive as well.

A lack of forgiveness can seriously affect your friendship with God because he doesn't bless you with grace so that you can hoard it. He expects you to pass it on, giving grace through forgiveness.

And don't worry—he'll help you forgive others.

Just be willing to give it a try.

GOD FIRST, STUFF SECOND

It's easy to flip that equation because stuff sits right in front of you and God feels far away.

Fire up your computer and temptation is just a few clicks away.

Watch a commercial for that sleek new car, kitchen, or cruise, and you're quickly coveting what you can't afford.

It's hard to remain mindful of God and his kingdom in this distracting world.

Yet consider this message God shared through a prophet: "Son of man, these leaders have set up idols in their hearts. They have embraced things that will make them fall into sin. Why should I listen to their requests?" (Ezekiel 14:3).

Grapple with *that* awhile. Ask yourself: What might I be valuing more highly than my friendship with God?

We ask not because we want you to feel guilty, but because distractions are sneaky. Has anything crept between you and God that you didn't notice as it happened?

REMEMBER WHO YOU'RE TALKING WITH

Yes, God's your friend...but he's unlike any of your other friends.

No one else equals God's all-in love for you. Or his faithfulness. Or his willingness to be available 24/7/365.

And then there's this: Unlike everyone else you know, he's *God.*

So approach him with great confidence and boldness. But mix that with a healthy respect and the full knowledge that you're the created and he's the Creator.

Give him the respect he deserves. And part of that respect is to honor him by doing what he tells you to do.

Maybe that's what John had in mind when he wrote this about prayer: "Dear friends, if we don't feel guilty, we can come to God with bold confidence. And we will receive from him whatever we ask because we obey him and do the things that please him" (1 John 3:21-22).

Does God consider you worthy of his time?

Absolutely. Even if you're less than perfect.

Don't believe that? Consider...

- Jesus spoke with Saul even as Saul was heading to Damascus to arrest Jesus' followers (Acts 9).
- God met Elijah while the prophet was so discouraged and fearful he wanted to die (1 Kings 19).
- A convicted criminal hanging on a cross heard Jesus answer his prayer, opening the very gates of heaven (Luke 23:42-43).

Prayers offered by woefully imperfect people, at the worst possible times, and yet answered by a perfect, loving, present God.

It's God's choice to call you his friend—and he sticks by his friends.

You're worthy of God's time, attention, and love because he's *made* you worthy.

Now if it were only possible to feel that way…

PAUSE TO PONDER

Describe a time you felt unworthy of coming to God in prayer. What was the situation? What, if anything, did you do about it?

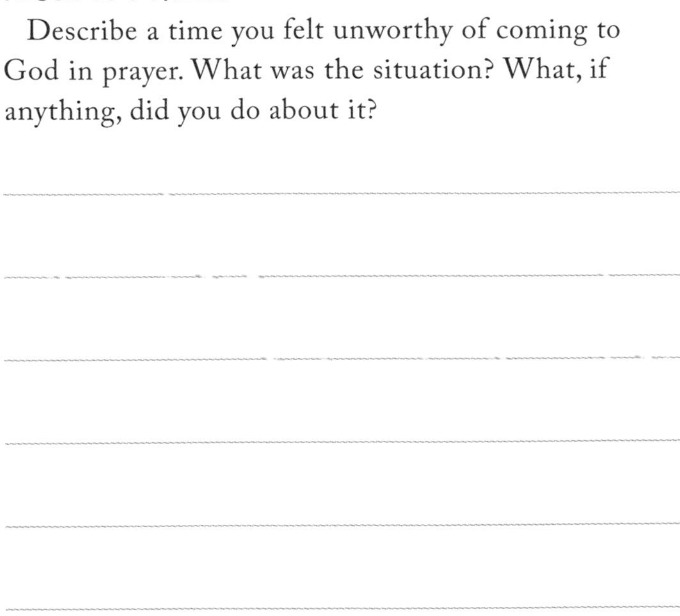

In what ways are you feeling worthy or unworthy of God's time and attention today? What might you do about it?

EXPERIMENT 1: Take the Test

Assuming you're an American, visit the website (uscis.gov/us-citizenship/naturalization-test) that describes the civics test immigrants must pass to become naturalized citizens.

Take the sample test.

Not an American? Find your country's equivalent test and take it.

If you're like most people—Americans, anyway—you'll score poorly. Yet no government agency will come knocking on your door to deport you.

Why? Because you're *already* a citizen. Your status doesn't depend on your test score, thankfully. You're worthy of being a citizen because you *are* a citizen.

And it's like that with your friendship with God. You're his friend, not because you've earned it but because he chose you to be his friend. He chose you knowing that you have some rough edges that need sanding, that sometimes when you pray you wander off into the weeds.

So talk with God about this: What matters most when it comes to being his friend? Is it how you pray, when you pray, or something else?

Listen carefully after asking. This is important stuff.

EXPERIMENT 2: Overdress for the Occasion

Invite a friend to get together for breakfast at the greasiest-spoon diner you can find. The one that never passes the health inspection the first time? That's it.

Dress as lavishly as possible for the breakfast. You can stop short of renting a tux or buying a formal, but get as close to perfection as your closet will allow.

Shine those shoes and starch that shirt. Press those undies until there's a crease.

See how your friend reacts when you show up looking as if your first stop after some bacon and eggs is a coronation. Just wait for your friend to ask why you're gussied up the way you are. Then ask, "How do you expect our conversation will be affected by the way I'm dressed, if at all? If I dressed way down instead, would that affect our conversation? Why or why not? When we've had a really good conversation, what has helped that happen?"

Maybe, just maybe, God doesn't expect us to show up for our conversations in full Mary Poppins mode (practically perfect in every way).

After breakfast ask God to reveal to you what helps the most to open up your conversations together. Then pause and listen.

See what he says.

EXPERIMENT 3: Graveside

Visit the grave of someone you love and have lost.

Trace the words etched in the tombstone with your fingers. Picture the face of the person who's been taken from you.

What would you give for one more conversation?

Would it matter to you if your loved one wasn't quite focused or had been disobedient? If he or she didn't believe the things you wanted that person to believe about you?

You'd overlook all of that in a second and move in close for a hug.

You'd be like a forgiving father who couldn't wait to see his prodigal son come around the bend and head toward the house.

Your son wouldn't need to earn your love or prove his worth. Your love would cover all that and more.

Talk with God about this as you wander around the cemetery awhile: Even though you know God's grace has made you worthy of his love, what will it take for you to *feel* worthy?

EXPERIMENT 4: Confession

Most Christians aren't very good at confessing their sins.

Not to God, and certainly not to each other.

But God didn't create you with the capacity to shoulder guilt forever, to carry it throughout your life. He's given you a place to dump guilt, and that's at his feet—so he can deal with it for you.

So do it: Confess your sins.

Out loud and in detail. Leave nothing out. Be specific.

Find a spot where you won't be overheard. Bring tissues. Bare your soul.

Then, once you've asked for forgiveness, brace yourself to experience a refreshing wave of freedom, cleansing your soul and lifting from your shoulders the weight of all you've done wrong.

Because it's one thing to know God's grace has made you worthy, loved, and forgiven.

It's a completely different thing to feel it.

"The eyes of
the Lord watch over
those who do right,
and his ears are open
to their prayers.
But the Lord turns
his face against
those who
do evil."

1 Peter 3:12

IF YOU WONDER HOW TO KNOW IF GOD'S ANSWERING...

Here's the conventional wisdom about how God answers prayers:

- He might answer yes, no, or "Not now."
- He answers in his own time; you can't push for an answer.
- He may respond in ways you don't easily see.
- His ways are higher than yours, so don't expect to understand.
- If what you're praying isn't in line with his will, he won't answer at all.

Quick question: Would you put up with that set of rules from any of your other friends?

Let's say you call a friend and ask her to join you for lunch next Tuesday. You might hear yes, no, or "I want to reschedule." Any of those answers are reasonable.

But waiting six months to respond? That doesn't work.

Answering in ways that aren't clear? What's the point?

Or getting an answer like "octopus"—something you simply don't understand?

In what universe does that sort of behavior make sense…and that sort of friendship survive?

We expect more from friends. We expect clear, timely communication, and if we don't get it, those friendships tend to fade as we become increasingly frustrated.

So why does it sometimes seem that God is simply not answering your prayers?

Keep in mind that, if prayer is part of how God is transforming you, he has no obligation to play Answer Man. You're in it together, sorting out how to navigate your life as you lean on God for wisdom and insight.

Sometimes *not* providing a quick, detailed plan for extracting you from a mess is exactly the right thing for God to do. You can learn more from one failure than 10 successes—and there's nothing like a crisis to refocus your attention on God.

And when God doesn't choose to miraculously heal your dying friend, he hasn't broken any promises. He never said people you love will get off this planet alive. While he's restored some people to health, he's under no obligation to do the same for everyone.

The truth is, his ways *are* higher than yours. You *won't* understand every decision God makes. But admit it: You don't fully understand half the decisions made by your other friends either.

Here's the bottom line about whether God is answering your prayers: Yes, he is. Not always on your recommended timeline or in ways you fully understand, but he's answering.

The harder question is whether you choose to trust him when you don't see any *evidence* that he's answering, when his answers aren't obvious.

Do you believe he's still faithful?

That's a question less about God's job performance than it is about the status of your friendship. Is it a trusting relationship or one based on God providing the goods whenever you ask him to?

When you wonder whether God is answering your prayers, consider these two suggestions that have helped others resolve that question:

First, pray with specificity.

If you ask for something, be specific about what you want so you can know if it happens.

When you pray, "God, surround Cheryl with the warmth of your love, and be with her in this time of economic uncertainty," good luck knowing if that prayer is answered.

But if you pray instead, "God, Cheryl needs a job—would you help her land an interview this week?" you'll see clearly how God responded.

So why don't most Christians get specific in their prayers?

One reason is that being specific feels as if we're bossing God around. You know, "Find me a primo parking spot, preferably one with money still in the meter, and have that ready about...oh...7:38 would be nice. Thanks. Hey, do you do valet parking?"

That's an awkward conversation to have with the God of the universe.

There's also fear we might not be praying in God's will. Maybe God doesn't want you in a great parking spot, so asking him to make that happen is wrong. Besides, do you really want to bother God with small requests like that?

So we hedge our bets by just praying that God's will be done. He knows best, and that's what Jesus prayed, right?

Except that's not *quite* what Jesus prayed.

Moments before Jesus prayed, "I want your will to be done, not mine" (Matthew 26:39), he asked God to spare him the suffering coming with his arrest and crucifixion. Jesus modeled a willingness to be both specific in our requests and humble in accepting God's answers—no matter what those answers are.

So it's okay to be specific, to ask for what you want. Jesus did it, and so can you.

But it's risky.

What if you ask for a specific outcome—one you think might be within God's will for a situation you care about—and you don't see God answer?

And there's the thornier reason you might decide not to get specific in your prayers: Can your faith handle failing to see God answer?

In the end it all comes back to this: your friendship with God.

If it's robust and vibrant, it can handle not always getting what you want. It can handle not getting an obvious answer. The trust is strong enough to carry you.

But if you're unsure about God, praying specifically is dangerous because you might not hear anything… or you may miss the subtle answer God provides.

Or God might respond with a thundering answer that rattles your world as he calls you off the bench into the thick of bringing about his will.

Second, be intentional about noticing God's answers.

There are lots of ways to notice and remember how God is answering your prayers: notes on a calendar, a list tucked in your pocket, or—our favorite—a prayer journal.

You'll experiment with prayer journaling soon. It's a way someone like you—someone who's busy and perhaps quick to forget what you've asked of God—can see how he's moving in your life.

And no, it won't be a boring duty. Not the way you'll do it.

PAUSE TO PONDER

If you pray in generalities, rather than specifically, why is that the case?

Is it a matter of how you've seen prayer modeled? Is it that you've never thought about being more specific?

Or is it that you're not willing to take the risk?

Describe your experience with specific prayer below.

Share your story with God. Ask him to speak to you—specifically—about how he'd like you to pray.

EXPERIMENT 1: Menu Specificity

Two options here: a fast-food drive-through window or a sit-down restaurant. Either works… though if you're with another person, the sit-down restaurant offers more opportunity to debrief the experience.

When you're asked what you want to order, don't be specific. Don't name any item or point to it on a menu. Rather, deliver some version of "Your will be done."

Be pleasant…but persistent. Keep deferring to the waitstaff to make your choices for you. See what happens.

Notice that this is someone who *wants* you to be specific. Who's *waiting* for you to be specific. Who's eager to give you what you want *if you'll just spell it out.*

And notice how frustrated the waitstaff becomes.

How might how you pray put God in the same spot as your waitstaff?

Caveat: Be sure when you say, "Your will be done," you're not holding the wine list or this will very quickly become an expensive experiment!

And tip well. Very well. Your waitstaff has earned it.

Once you've given this a try, jot a few notes about the experience. How did it go, and in what ways might this experience change how you pray?

EXPERIMENT 2: Too Small to Care

If you have a young child, this will be easy. No kids in the house? Then call a friend and arrange to borrow one for a few hours—preferably a child who likes you.

Promise an outing to a kid-friendly restaurant.

Your goal is to have a conversation with your short guest (you are picking up the check, right?) and to do your best to pay close attention to everything the child says. As in, *everything.*

So ask lots of questions and follow-up questions. Ask for details. Drill down into stories. Explore bunny trails. Be the best grown-up listener the child has ever had the pleasure of sharing a plate of french fries with.

Here are a dozen questions and comments to get the conversational ball rolling:

- What's something that made you happy this week? sad? angry? scared?
- What's something you do really well?
- What's something you used to think was real but now know isn't?
- Ketchup was used as a medicine in the 1800s. What do you think it could cure?
- If you could have just one superpower, what would you pick—and why?
- What's something you'd like to do for fun but is too scary?
- If you found a hundred dollars, what would you do with it?
- Would you rather eat a snake or a horse? Why?

- If your teeth had to be a different color, what color would you choose?
- Would you rather wear your shirt or your pants backward for a day?
- What do you like most about your school? least?
- Tell me all about your best friend and what you do together.

Once you've dropped off the child, jot a few notes about how the experiment went. Was it tiring or invigorating? And given that you wanted to be a great listener, what details seemed too small to care about? Any of them?

Given that God's determined to be a great listener, what details in your life do you think he considers too small to care about? Any of them?

> "And we are confident that he hears us whenever we ask for anything that pleases him. And since we know he hears us when we make our requests, we also know that he will give us what we ask for."
>
> *1 John 5:14–15*

PRAYER ADJUSTMENT: JESUS DIDN'T GET EVERYTHING HE ASKED FOR EITHER

It's worth another mention: Jesus didn't always get what he asked for.

While praying in Gethsemane, Jesus asked God three times for an easier path than the one leading from the garden to the cross to the tomb.

Three times.

And the answer was no.

You'd think if anyone could sway God, it would be…God. Because Jesus *is* God, right? Fully divine, fully human, fully…confusing, at least to those of us without theology degrees.

Which raises an elephant-in-the-room question: Why did Jesus pray at all? What was the point?

People who have given that question a great deal of thought suggest there are at least three reasons Jesus often prayed for and with others:

- He was setting an example. Jesus' followers noticed that Jesus didn't pray like anyone else they knew. There was an intimacy to Jesus' prayers; prayer was an intrinsic part of a relationship, not a routine. The disciples, good Jewish boys raised to pray since they were children, were so touched by what they heard that they asked Jesus to teach them how to pray.
- Jesus is fully human. Yes, Jesus is fully divine—but he's also fully human. And when he was on earth, the human part of Jesus cried out for a connection with his heavenly Father.
- God is hungry for relationship. The very nature of the Trinity is relational, and it's no surprise that there's ongoing joy in that community. Of course Jesus remains in constant communion with the Father and Holy Spirit—it's who Jesus is.

And then there's this: Jesus' words "I want your will to be done, not mine" make it abundantly clear that the human part of Jesus knows that God is in charge.

We ask...and bask in the love of his friendship.
We ask...and trust the wisdom in his response.
We ask...and walk the path he opens before us.

IF YOU'VE NEVER TRIED A PRAYER JOURNAL...

Maybe you're a fan of journaling. No day is complete until you've summed it up in a page or two or 10. Were the police to ask you what you were doing three years ago on August 16th, you could tell them not only where you were but also what you had for lunch.

But that's you.

The rest of us launch into journaling with a sense of dread. Daily entries become a duty; we feel obligated to write something even if nothing memorable happened that day.

There's a reason that in every thrift store there's a shelf groaning under the weight of journals with the first four or five pages torn out. That's how far the original owners got before they gave up the fight.

So if you're a journal aficionado, welcome home. You're going to love this.

But if you've struggled with journaling before or don't especially like to write, you may be tempted to pass over this section.

Please don't, for two reasons:

First, this isn't journaling as you've experienced it before. There's no expectation that you'll curl up daily with a cup of tea, a spare hour, and legible penmanship. This is journaling for the rest of us.

And second, you'll just run into journaling again because there are blank journaling pages in the back of this book. Resistance is futile, so you might as well do something about it now.

Besides, the point of prayer journaling isn't to write literary reminiscences about your garden so, years from now, you can look back and be reminded of how well the gardenias did.

The point is to keep track of how God is answering your prayers. And you can do that with a scrawled line of text, a photo, a headline torn from a newspaper, or a doodle. Whatever jogs your memory when you next open your journal.

And here's the best part about a prayer journal: You're in charge of the journal; it's not in charge of you. *You* decide when and where to open it and how best to use it.

If you choose to take the time to write out prayers, there's real benefit there. The act of writing slows you down and can help you focus. You can write and revise, sharpening and distilling what you most want to say to God.

And you can pause to listen, making a note of what you hear in response.

If you'd rather use your journal as a canvas for drawing or cartooning, that's fine, too. Again, whatever helps you pray and recall what you've prayed—that's the right way to use your journal.

So feel free to experiment. Try writing, drawing, even origami. There's no way to get this wrong as long as your journal prompts you to be mindful of what you pray and attentive to how God answers. You'll have the opportunity to look back at something you prayed about even years before and see how God used you, others, and circumstances to respond to your prayers.

Any parent of grown children knows that some prayers—like those about a child's future—take years to answer.

And we've added a unique feature to your journal pages. We invite you to make note of how you feel throughout the process.

How you feel when you pray a prayer.

How you feel when you hear from God.

How you feel when you and God have a conversation about what has—or hasn't—happened.

Talk with God about all those moments—because that's what friends do.

And please know that you can use this journal to do more than document your requests. If you're feeling especially grateful, tell God that—and make a note. Feeling sad or scared, but not sure why? God's your friend and will want to know about that, too.

PAUSE TO PONDER

Right now, at this moment, how do you feel about using these prayer journal pages?

If you're hesitating at all, why? What past experiences or present circumstances are getting in the way?

If you were to give this a try, what might be the best thing to come out of it for you?

EXPERIMENT 1: Kick the Tires

When wandering around a car lot, looking for a new car, people sometimes say they're "kicking the tires." They're looking—but not committed. All they're ready for is a test drive.

Let's kick the tires of this whole prayer journal thing, too...but not with God. Do it with a friend, instead, one with whom you can talk openly.

Call your friend and ask to get together for a walk or a cup of coffee—anything simple.

Before you meet, jot the date in the top space on the Sample Prayer Journal Page on page 82. And knowing full well your friend isn't God, complete the sentence "Here's why I'd like to talk with you and how I feel right now."

For example, if you want to talk with your friend about how to deal with an upcoming job interview, fill that in as well as how you're feeling about getting together with him or her.

After you and your friend talk, pause to fill out Part 2. Your friend can order a second cup of coffee or do another lap around the track as you do this.

Then talk about Part 3—after explaining the journal page and confirming you're well aware your friend isn't God.

After you've gone through the process once, with a friend you can see, are you willing to go through the same process with God?

Jot your thoughts about that below.

EXPERIMENT 2: Memory Tester

Of course you don't need a journal to remember what you've prayed. Of course your mind is a steel trap, and you miss nothing.

So let's take a little trip down memory lane and see how far we get.

Jot your answers to the following questions:

The last time you were in church (Christmas and Easter don't count), what was the sermon about?

List the contents of your car's glove compartment.

Without looking, how many buttons are on the front of your shirt?

How much cash are you carrying in your wallet, purse, or pocket?

What's engraved on the back of a $5 bill?

Given the results of this pop quiz, do you think it's possible a journal might help you remember what you pray? And notice when God responds?

The prosecution rests, your honor. You'll find blank journal pages beginning on page 146.

SAMPLE PRAYER JOURNAL PAGE

Part 1

Date: ____________________

God, here's why I'd like to talk with you and how I feel right now...

Part 2

Date: ______________

Here's how I think you answered, God, and how I feel about your response...

Part 3

Date: ________________

God, let's talk about what happened. I'll tell you how I feel about you, and you tell me how you feel about me, okay?

(For more Prayer Journal pages, see the back of this book. You have our permission to copy them for your personal use. You're welcome!)

JUST RELAX

If you've ever strapped on a parachute, jumped off the high dive, or stepped on stage for the first time, you've discovered this truth: Someone saying, "Just relax" doesn't relax you.

Sometimes it does the opposite.

Even so, you can greatly enhance your prayer life by taking this advice: Just relax.

Prayer isn't like arranging an audience with the president or prime minister, with just one shot to say what you want to say. You're talking with God, a friend who has infinite time, patience, and love for you.

It's okay if you fumble a bit. It's even okay if you pause, close your eyes, concentrate as hard as you can on hearing God speak to you, and get…nothing.

It's okay because maybe it's not time for an answer yet. Or the answer will be coming another way. Or not hearing *is* the answer.

When you don't get an immediate response from God, it's not a reflection of your spiritual maturity. Make a note in your prayer journal and move on.

And while you're at it, here's some great advice from Rick Lawrence, author of *The Jesus-Centered Life:*

"When it comes to hearing God, I tell people to imagine themselves as a catcher in a baseball game. They're wearing a catcher's mitt, crouched behind the plate, and 60 feet 6 inches away is a pitcher who's going to sizzle a pitch their direction.

"The only 'work' a catcher does is hold out a mitt for the ball to hit.

"When you're listening for God, you don't have that much work to do. You stay in a posture that's invitational and open, and you believe there's a pitch coming to you.

"So just hold up your mitt and say, 'Pitcher, throw me a strike.' And wait for the ball to arrive because it's coming."

Freeing, isn't it? Scrunching your brow and trying harder and harder to hear God's voice isn't required. You can just relax and be open to hearing from him, ready to catch God's pitch.

Because a pitch *is* coming your way.

PAUSE TO PONDER

How much pressure do you feel when you're praying—and why do you think you feel that pressure?

What exactly are the pressure points you experience? Are they more about praying in the right way so you're heard by God or more about hearing God's answer?

Talk with God about your responses. What does he have to say about them?

EXPERIMENT 1: Tell God a Joke

Sometimes friends just like to share a good laugh.

Yes, God is the almighty creator, and giving him the respect and awe he deserves is wise. But he's also called you his friend, and making space for that relationship is at the very center of his heart for you.

So do what friends do now and then: Risk sharing a smile with God.

Tell him a joke.

If you've got one you think is appropriate, by all means go with that. But if the very idea of asking the God of the universe to sit expectantly waiting for you to deliver a punchline gives you humor constipation, here's one for you to use:

A man awoke one morning to discover that, during the night, a flood had surrounded his house. The rising waters quickly engulfed the first floor and then swiftly rose to fill the second, forcing the man up onto the roof.

There he sat, surveying a scene of complete devastation.

And still the waters rose, sending him inching ever higher up the shingles.

"God," he prayed, "I've served you faithfully for years, and I believe you'll save me from this predicament. Just as you rescued Daniel from lions, I trust you for a miracle to rescue me."

He was still praying when a neighbor clinging to a floating garage door drifted near. The neighbor urged the stranded man to swim over; the door would hold them both.

"Hardly miraculous," thought the stranded man, who waved his neighbor away.

Next came a friend in a rowboat, desperately straining against the current to maneuver his boat beside the quickly sinking roof.

"God is a mighty God," thought the man who was now just inches from the chimney. "He wouldn't send a rowboat in place of a miracle."

Unable to keep the boat in place, the friend was swept away toward a watery horizon.

Now balanced on the top of his chimney, the man saw a helicopter quickly approaching. It hovered over the stranded man, dangling a rope within his reach.

"I'll wait for God to intervene," thought the stranded man. When he didn't grab hold of the lifeline, the helicopter banked away, off to rescue more willing flood victims.

The man drowned, of course. And when he stood before God demanding to know why God hadn't answered his prayer, God threw up his hands in frustration.

"I sent a garage door, a rowboat, and a helicopter," God said. "What exactly were you expecting?"

Yes, you've heard that joke before. So has God. But you haven't told it to him—and when you do, you're taking your friendship to a relaxing spot you've not visited with God yet.

So tell God the joke. Really.

Then talk this over with God: How did that feel? See what God has to say about your response (and your joke-telling).

EXPERIMENT 2: Morning Commute

The next time you head to work or the grocery store, invite God to come along.

But be deliberate: Before you jump in the car, open the passenger side door. Hold it open long enough for God to get in, and then close the door for him. (Hey, he's *God.* It's a good idea to be polite.)

As you drive, have a conversation about life. The traffic. Weather. How the kids are doing or how unreasonable your boss has been lately.

Just...have a conversation.

Talk, listen, be aware of the topics that God wants to address with you as you two make your way to wherever you're going.

When you arrive, invite God to go in with you. You wouldn't really expect him to remain in the car waiting, would you?

When you've finished, make a few notes on the following page. How did it go...and are you willing to do this again?

And just out of curiosity, did imagining having God belted in beside you change how you drove?

IF YOU CAN'T PRAY LIKE EVERYONE ELSE...

There's no shortage of formulas telling you how to pray.

There's "ACTS": Adoration, Confession, Thanksgiving, Supplication.

And "TRIP": Thanks, Regret, Intercession, Purpose.

Toss "PARTS" into the mix, too: Praise, Ask, Repent, Thanks, Sharing.

And our all-time favorite —"WOOPS": Worship, Obedience, Opportunities, Praise, Supplication.

Don't misunderstand; these aren't bad in and of themselves. A short formula can help you answer the question "Now that I'm praying, what do I talk about next?"

But if you believe prayer is about relationship, relying on a formula won't be helpful for long. How many of your conversations with friends need a formula to direct the discussion?

Formulas quickly feel artificial and stifling...as does praying the same way every other person prays.

So here's a thought: Why not pray the way you're wired?

Our friend Jeff struggled in school, especially when it came time to doing in-class reading. "I'm just not designed to sit still," he says. "I'm always up and moving, so just being in school was hard enough. Having to sit at a desk and read page after page was torture."

It wasn't until Jeff was an adult that he discovered he could actually walk around while reading. And do math. And do practically everything else that his high school had insisted be done at a desk.

Once he gave himself permission to learn the way he learns best and to express himself in a way that felt comfortable, his horizons expanded, and his career blossomed. He became enormously successful—and stays in pretty good shape, by the way.

Here's how you may have been told to pray: Reverently. Eyes closed. Head bowed. Hushed tones. And perhaps it was also communicated this was a description of how prayer is *supposed* to look.

This would have come as something of a shock to David, who joyfully danced before God (2 Samuel 6:14) and then sat down later to pray (2 Samuel 7:18).

Or Jonah, who managed to squeak out a prayer from inside the belly of a large fish (Jonah 2:1-2).

The Bible portrays people praying while kneeling (Ephesians 3:14), lying facedown (2 Chronicles 20:18), with their hands outstretched (1 Kings 8:22-23), and while standing (1 Samuel 1:26).

Again, there's nothing wrong with closing your eyes and bowing your head—*if* that works for you. But if you're Jeff, you won't be praying long if that's how you have to do it.

So try praying the way you're wired. There's ample evidence God will welcome your honoring, respectful prayer no matter how you lay it before him.

This, of course, assumes you *know* how you're wired.

Educators often talk about three different ways learners take in and process information—three ways kids are wired (stay tuned—we'll tell you what they are in a few minutes). Teachers pay attention to learning styles because they matter when you're trying to help a kid master math.

But your learning style doesn't only affect how it's best to communicate with you. It also dictates how *you* prefer to share information with *others*...others like God.

In situations like prayer.

Your wiring affects what communication feels natural and what feels forced. What flows easily and what requires effort to translate into a different style.

Simply put, if you're connecting with God in a way that reflects how he wired you, you'll have a stronger connection. So let's look at those three styles of wiring and consider which one reminds you of...you.

Because—spoiler alert—we're going to ask you to experiment with how to pray in each of these three styles.

KINESTHETIC WIRING

Our friend Jeff is a great example of kinesthetic, hands-on wiring. As a child he was that fidgety kid who got his hand slapped for touching things, and as an adult he finds he still prefers doing over observing.

Yes, he can navigate the other two learning styles (almost all of us can), but he feels most comfortable when he's moving, building, sketching, doing almost anything except sitting and listening.

If you're heavily kinesthetic, you've probably already found a way to turn this book into a drum kit, second base in a softball game, or a tool that helped level out that short leg on the dining room table.

Thanks for retrieving it and continuing to read, by the way.

VISUAL WIRING

If you're visually wired, you take in information best by seeing it or picturing it in your mind as it's described to you.

Graphs, charts, and pictures make sense to you. You're constantly looking, perpetually noticing what's going on in your world. You're probably also someone with a good sense of when something looks just a little bit…off. If you've ever straightened the pictures hanging in a friend's house, consider yourself visual.

And this probably isn't the only book you own—you love soaking in information through your eyes. You may enjoy connecting with others the same way; you're the one who still handwrites notes to friends.

And journaling? Assuming you're allowed to draw as well as write, the idea that you'll be journaling makes you feel all tingly inside—in a good way.

AUDITORY WIRING

If this is you, you're probably fairly comfortable with closing your eyes and listening as someone prays aloud. You may be wondering what the problem is with people whose minds drift off during meditative, low-light prayer times at church. If they'd just buckle down and *listen,* they'd be fine, right?

Because you have exactly zero trouble listening. You *love* listening—to music, to good stories, to pretty much everything.

And the possibility that you could actually hear God's voice speaking to you leaves you breathless. How cool would it be to *actually hear the voice of God*?

You can't wait.

So a quick question: Of these three styles—kinesthetic, visual, and auditory—which feels most like you?

Granted, you probably live in all three worlds—there's a great deal of overlap in most everyone. But one style is likely your default setting, the way you most prefer to take in and organize information. Which of those descriptions would your friends point to and say, "That is *so* you"?

There's no wrong answer because, however you're wired, you're God's handiwork. He made you as you are, crafting your unique combination of strengths, weaknesses, quirks, and hiccups. You're exactly what he had in mind.

And he's eager to connect with you.

So let's experiment with praying in ways that will resonate with each of the three learning and communication styles. It's likely one or two of the experiments will be epic failures, and your experiences won't enhance your prayer time whatsoever.

That's okay. You're sorting out what *will* work well—so you can then do more of it.

But before you launch into experiments…

PAUSE TO PONDER

Some people spend their entire lives wishing they'd been designed differently. They wish they had different hair, bodies, talents, or even learning styles.

Which means they lose out on the wonder of simply being who God made them to be.

So we have to ask: Which of the three styles seems most like you—and how do you feel about that?

If you're less than satisfied with how God wired you, what's shaped your discontent? And what might help you make peace with who you are?

EXPERIMENT 1: Sculpting

Find a friendly 5-year-old and borrow some modeling dough. Even better, buy some for yourself—because you may decide to keep it.

Find a comfortable spot, pop open the container, and create a shape that reflects how you're feeling.

If you're feeling lonely, you might fashion a human figure with a hole through its middle. Feeling happy? A sunny smiley face says it all.

Then create a shape or two that reflects a question you have for God. As you sculpt, ask God to speak into your creativity, to guide your fingers as you craft something that speaks to both of you.

Continue the conversation wherever it takes you.

Before mashing the modeling dough back into a container, place one of your sculptures where it will remind you to look for God's ongoing answer to the question you posed. It'll be a reminder that continuing the conversation with God is always an option, too.

Quick tip: Your sculpture will enjoy a mold-free future if you pop it onto a foil-covered cookie sheet in a 200-degree oven for about 10 minutes. After 10 minutes turn off the oven, and let the sculpture sit until the oven cools.

When you've finished this experience, talk with God about how it went. Could you give yourself permission to see this as prayer? Is it something you might do again?

EXPERIMENT 2: Magazine Prayers

For this experiment you'll need a short stack of magazines. We headed to our local library where they toss extra and out-of-date magazines in a box, free for the taking.

Find a spot at home where you can relax. Ask God if there's anything he wants to show you. Tell him you're ready and willing to receive whatever he has for you.

Then thumb through the magazines.

Don't let yourself be snagged by articles—keep your focus on the photos and the headlines. When something you see sparks your interest or stirs a feeling, rip out that page and set it aside.

After a few minutes of scanning and tearing, glance through the pages you've torn out.

Ask God to help you understand why the photos and words you selected touched you and what message they might carry from God.

When you've finished this experience, talk with God about how it went. What, if anything, did you discover? Is it something you might do again?

EXPERIMENT 3: Doodle Prayers

You'll need a pen or pencil and a short stack of paper, so gather those before finding a spot where you're comfortable doodling and drawing.

Briefly ask God to help you clear your mind of distractions. Ask him to reveal himself to you through what you draw and to enter into this experience with you.

Then…doodle away.

As people come to mind, draw stick figures (and if you can do full sketches, that's fine, too!) and pray for those people. As situations float through your mind, capture them on the page in a quick word or drawing.

Don't worry about revising your work. There's more paper at your elbow, and what you draw won't be hanging on any refrigerator doors unless you post it there yourself. Just find a flow and remain there, drawing what comes to mind.

When you feel yourself drawn back to the present, talk with God about what you've drawn and written. What's there—and what does God have to say about it?

And decide: Is this something you might want to do again?

EXPERIMENT 4: Long-Distance Prayers

David danced before God, and if that speaks to you, by all means go for it. (You just might want to check before springing it on the folks at the sunrise Easter service.)

But at home it's all fair game. You can dance, sing, spin, or praise God as you stretch and strain through a workout routine.

For our experiment, though, just take a hike.

Whenever it's convenient, take a brief walk through the neighborhood. As you do, stay aware of your surroundings but also give yourself over to prayer. Ask God what he might like to say as the two of you walk together—and let the steady rhythm of your steps create a peaceful sense of well-being.

Your goal isn't covering distance; it's being with God. So if something snags your attention—a weed pushing up through a crack in the sidewalk, an elderly person sitting alone on a porch stoop—feel free to stop and engage. After all, God might be wanting to speak to you through an image that springs to your mind or a conversation with someone.

When you've finished this experience, debrief it with God. Did you see your walk as prayer? Is this something you might do again?

EXPERIMENT 5: God's Voice

Go to a spot where you can stop, close your eyes, and listen to the sounds of nature.

A breeze rustling through leaves. The trill of birds. Bright water rippling over stones.

Close your eyes and listen intently.

Open your heart and breathe deeply.

Ask God to speak to you in the sounds you hear. How do you hear his voice? What might he be saying to you?

Find a place full of bustle and commotion. A park bench near a busy street or a seat on a subway.

Again, close your eyes and listen carefully.

Ask God to speak to you, to help you hear him in the voices and sounds that wash over you.

How do you hear his voice? What might he be saying to you?

EXPERIMENT 6: Follow the Music

Fire up your online music account or listen to an instrumental CD that moves you.

Classical music, electronic tracks, acoustic guitar solos, even your local zither band's offerings—whatever music seems to wrap itself around you and lift you up and away from your everyday concerns.

As the music plays, ask God to speak to you in some way, to meet you in the music.

What thoughts come to mind? What faces appear? What nudges do you feel?

Whatever you experience, prayerfully follow along, asking God to make himself known.

Once you've finished this experience, talk it over with God.

How did it go—and is this something you'd do again?

WHAT DID YOU DISCOVER?

Take a moment to assess which of the six prayer experiences resonated with you most. In which settings were you more easily able to slip into a conversation with God? When were you best able to hear God?

If it was experiments 1 and 4, you're likely kinesthetic.

Experiments 2 and 3? You're visual.

And if experiments 5 and 6 are where you found your sweet spot, perhaps praying in more auditory ways will be helpful to you.

No matter where you landed, God has the ability to connect with you in the way you're wired.

So bow your head, close your eyes, and meditate.

Or lift your face to a star-strewn night sky and marvel at God's greatness.

Or listen to the call of wolves in the wild and know that you're safe in the love of your Father.

It's all good.

So long as you and God are talking, it's always good.

"Devote yourselves to prayer with an alert mind and a thankful heart."

Colossians 4:2

“Don’t worry about anything; instead, pray about everything. Tell God what you need, and thank him for all he has done.”

Philippians 4:6

IF EVEN THE LORD'S PRAYER FEELS FLAT...

They're among the most quoted words ever. They're drawn from the Bible, the most popular, most frequently printed book in history. And they're recited in countless churches around the globe every week.

But many of us are sort of...over them.

They've become wallpaper, hanging there for so long we hardly notice them any longer.

Is it okay that the Lord's Prayer no longer moves you when you read or recite it? After all, it's the perfect prayer—one Jesus himself prayed.

It helps to remember the context in which Jesus offered up this prayer.

He was having a conversation with his disciples. Like all good Jewish boys, they'd been trained early how to pray, so Jesus' disciples had the fundamentals down pat. They knew what to say, when to say it, and how to strike the proper attitude while praying.

But when Jesus prayed, they caught a whiff of something different. They sensed an intimacy, something that wasn't really part of their training.

So they were curious. When one of them finally said, "Lord, teach us to pray, just as John taught his disciples" (Luke 11:1), Jesus agreed—and provided a sample prayer. It's essentially the same one he shared during his Sermon on the Mount.

That sample prayer is what came to be known as the Lord's Prayer. Jesus never said he intended it to be used verbatim in church services. Or to be recited by his followers in place of their own prayers, in their own words.

But because this *is* Jesus' model prayer, we can probably learn a few things that might influence how we pray. So let's take a quick look—without spending a dozen pages analyzing every phrase for deeper meaning.

Jesus launched into his prayer by saying, "Father, may your name be kept holy."

There's great affection in those words as Jesus declares that he loves his Father and honors God just as God is: holy. God's perfect as is, with no blemish to heal or issue to address.

That's affirmation we, too, can offer to God.

Then Jesus said, "May your Kingdom come soon."

Whatever God wants, Jesus is all in. He's on board. There's humility there, as well as a deep yearning to see God fully known and worshipped.

Which isn't a bad way to think of your prayer life—as an attempt to know God more deeply. And when you see God clearly, it's hard to do anything *but* worship him.

Jesus continued, asking for food—a very practical, physical need. Consider this permission for you to do the same, to come to God with concerns as they arise. Paying the rent, having your car chug along for another year—God cares about your concerns because he cares about you.

Jesus then asked God to forgive sins but linked that forgiveness to our own willingness to forgive others. Jesus made it clear that if you can't give others what you've received, you and God need to talk about that.

Jesus closed by asking God not to let us yield to temptation. That faithfulness comes by remaining firmly attached to Jesus, by the way. No one can muster resistance to temptation through sheer willpower.

So again: It all comes down to relationship. Friendship with God runs throughout Jesus' model prayer. It can run through your prayers, too, because God has called you his friend.

PAUSE TO PONDER

For some, Jesus' model prayer becomes difficult the moment he says "Father."

Because some people have fathers who have been anything but kind or understanding. Anything but loving.

So why would they tell their fathers about their lives? About feeling hurt, confused, or vulnerable? What good could come of it?

Perhaps to some extent that describes you.

You, too, are wary when thinking of God as your Father because your earthly father was decidedly imperfect. What you've experienced with your earthly father has colored how willing you are to embrace your heavenly Father—and that's built a wall between you and God.

Yes, he's God. But he can be God at a distance—no getting too close, thank you very much.

We'd like to suggest this: If you want your prayers to be anything besides flat, close the distance between you and God. It's time to risk relationship.

Until then, even Jesus' words won't move you.

So give this some thought: How has your relationship with your earthly father, or other men who have raised you, influenced your view of your heavenly Father?

Think about it and then, if you're willing, ask God to share his thoughts about it with you as well. Believe it or not, God is actually the perfect Father, the one who's an ideal model for anyone who wants to fill the father role. He's worth hearing.

Jot down what you think and hear:

How would you answer the disciples' question?

When they asked Jesus to teach them to pray, the disciples asked exactly the right person. Fully human, fully God...he fully understood both ends of the prayer process.

You're a bit less informed, but still: How would you answer if someone asked *you* how to pray? If you had just a minute or two to respond, what would you say is most important to know—and do?

Without over-thinking your response, jot it down.

EXPERIMENT 1: Reflective Prayer

The goal here isn't to give you a fresh appreciation of Jesus' model prayer.

It's for you to have a fresh appreciation of your *own* prayers and of the God who's in this with you.

If you never again say or read Jesus' model prayer, that's okay. No matter what your Sunday school or confirmation class teacher told you, the ability to recite it isn't mandatory for admittance to heaven.

But try this experiment to see if perhaps Jesus' words might have new meaning for you.

You'll need to have Jesus' prayer handy, so get a Bible. Find a quiet spot where you can read aloud without being disturbed.

Read the prayer aloud (Matthew 6:9-13), one verse at a time, pausing after each verse.

Ask God: If you were to answer this prayer *in my life*, how might that look? What might it mean for how I live?

Allow God time to speak to you as you move through the prayer. What thoughts come to mind? What images drift into your awareness?

When you've finished, consider how such deliberate, guided prayer felt. Is it something you'd consider doing again?

PRAYER ADJUSTMENT: LOSE THE LINGO

There are times to carefully weigh every word you say. In court. During marriage proposals. Perhaps while explaining why there's a new dent in the car's fender.

But when you deliberate over each word you use while praying or find yourself using stilted "prayer language," it can quickly interfere with why you're praying at all: to connect with God.

If you're cautious in speaking with God because you're keenly aware that he's the creator, so powerful he can breathe life into clay and spin entire solar systems into existence, you're right to be awed.

You're right to respect the infinite power and might of God.

Just be sure your respect doesn't distance you from his friendship.

And if you're using special words you wouldn't use elsewhere—"thee" and "thou," for instance—you've put yourself in an awkward spot because you're praying in a foreign language.

Middle Ages English isn't especially user-friendly today, especially when you get to contemporary issues. For instance, "In thy great wisdom grant unto thy servant speedy tech support for this, mine laptop, O Lord" just doesn't roll off the tongue.

You've put yourself in a spot where you have to split your focus between what you're saying and how you're saying it...which leaves little room for listening.

Do this. The next time you pray, do so aloud—and record the conversation. Simply set your phone on the "record" function, and then forget about it until you're finished praying.

In a day or two, when you have some distance from the prayer, listen to it. Does it sound like you're talking with a friend? Are you using language you'd never use anywhere else?

If that's the case, reconsider. It's okay to come to God as you'd come to any friend. The best friendships always include a healthy dollop of respect—and affection and joy.

IF YOU'RE NOT SURE WHETHER YOU'RE HEARING GOD'S VOICE OR SOMETHING ELSE...

Recognizing God's voice in the cacophony of other voices speaking into your life is a big, big deal.

When you're praying and a thought or image comes to mind, how do you know it's God speaking and not just a memory drifting into your consciousness? Or perhaps it's your own voice or—far worse—another spiritual entity making itself known.

How do you know if that nudge you're feeling is really from God?

Bottom line: You don't, not until you grow so accustomed to God's voice that you can pick it out of the crowd. And that happens the same way you get to know anyone's voice: by being with that person enough to know the person intimately.

Though there are some things you can do to help you recognize God's voice.

First, if you're confident that God has given you authority on earth to address spiritual matters, make use of that authority.

When you're praying say, "In the name of Jesus, I declare that I will hear only God's voice as I listen. I silence my own voice and the voices of anything or anyone other than God."

It can be equally helpful to ask God to let you respond emotionally to what you hear in prayer. If you're hearing God, ask that his peace pour through you. If what you hear is from yourself or anything else, ask God to alert you through a deep unease, a hard anxiety.

Because you can be sure of this: If you're hearing God's voice, it will always be loving. God may have some challenging things to tell you, but they'll always be loving, always said for your ultimate good.

You'll also find that God often speaks to you with a sense of playfulness, with a deep calm tinged with humor. He already knows how the challenges you're facing will resolve; he isn't worried about them nearly as much as you are.

If you believe you've been given something to do as a response to prayer, you can also pause to ask:

- Does it sound like something God would do? He never contradicts his own nature; does the action you think you're to take reflect his values?
- Does what you'll do lift up and praise Jesus?
- Is what you'll do biblical? Is it consistent with what he's asked others to do in the Bible's account of God's interaction with mankind?
- Does it make sense to other believers? Ask a few and see what they say.

But even after all that, it's likely to come down to this: taking it on faith and taking the risk.

If the idea that prayer is a dialogue, a healthy communication between you and God, is new to you, and if you're not someone who's experienced direct communication from God in the past, move slowly. Start small, not with the largest decisions of your life but rather with less momentous decisions for which you'd like God's input.

Then step out and see if you've heard God.

Yes? Wonderful—you're now better able to hear him next time.

No? Keep listening—because he *is* speaking to you.

PAUSE TO PONDER

Describe a time you believe you heard God speak in response to prayer:

If that's never happened to you, ask God what would help you be ready to hear from him in that way.

EXPERIMENT 1: Gotcha

Go someplace noisy and crowded, preferably a place where there's a great deal of hustle and bustle.

A cafeteria at noon. A sports event where the crowd's engaged and enthusiastic. The lobby of a train station or airport.

Place yourself where you can listen in on conversations without attracting the attention of anyone with a badge or rolled-up newspaper.

Close your eyes, pick out a voice speaking somewhere around you and just—listen. Zero in on that voice. See how long and how well you can follow what that person is saying.

You're practicing hearing one voice among many, screening out distractions as you go.

You're also eavesdropping, which is something your mom said never to do. You can quietly help the people you're listening to by praying for them. And be open to the idea that God may have placed you where you are because he wants you to do more than pray. Perhaps you're where you are to meet a need, too.

"My sheep
listen to my voice;
I know them, and they
follow me. I give them eternal
life, and they will never perish.
No one can snatch them away
from me, for my Father has given
them to me, and he is more
powerful than anyone else.
No one can snatch them
from the Father's hand.
The Father and I are one."

—JESUS
John 10:27-30

IF "PRAY WITHOUT CEASING" FEELS IMPOSSIBLE...

Of course it's impossible. At least, it's impossible if your idea of praying is to close your eyes and talk at God.

Good luck driving to work while doing *that,* although you'll certainly inspire other drivers to pray while you're in their vicinity.

When Paul writes, "Never stop praying" (1 Thessalonians 5:17), he's not encouraging a nonstop monologue aimed in God's direction. He's urging his readers to be ever aware of God in their lives, to move through their days constantly prepared to invite God into whatever is happening.

To always remain fully conscious of their relationship with God.

Apparently God isn't to be relegated to "Sunday friend" status. Or "when I'm happy" status or "only when I'm in trouble" status.

He's your friend always. Your constant companion.

That's prayer without ceasing, and it's very, very possible...though it may require a shift in your thinking.

Perhaps you've got prayer all organized and in a box—it's something you do at mealtimes, when you're in church, during your daily devotions. And that's working fine for you, truth be told.

Except if prayer hasn't turned stale yet, it will soon because that's not how relationships grow.

If your best friend, the one who's always texting or emailing, was told there were specific times that checking in was permitted and that otherwise you weren't to be interrupted, how well would that conversation end?

So pull prayer out of any box you have it in—and we've got a suggestion for how to grow in your ability to do that.

Following is a list of triggers—moments you're likely to encounter throughout your day that can help you get in the habit of praying at unexpected times. The goal isn't to simply add more times you're required to pray, but to help you be aware that opportunities to pray can take you by surprise.

So feel free to try these dozen triggers, but only after you promise not to turn them into something you *must* do. They're offered to help free you, not burden you.

So…you promise? Really? Because if you don't…

Okay, then. Here you go…

- When you meet a new person, quickly ask God, "Is there something you want me to say to this person?"
- When you're stopped at a red light, glance around you at other drivers. If someone's stressed, pray for peace of mind. If someone's using a cellphone, pray for that person's safety—and yours. If *you're* on your cellphone, repent.
- When you use water, thank God for that gift in a world where so many don't have access to clean water.
- When you hit the ATM, pray for the poor of the world…and your own town.
- When you glance at a clock, thank God for the gift of today.
- When you finish eating, thank God for that gift of nourishment.
- When you see your reflection, ask God to make you a reflection of his love.
- When you open social media, ask God who you might encourage with a quick email or message.

- When you walk into work, thank God for your job and the people you can serve through your job.
- Before opening a text from a friend, ask God if there's something he has for your friend—and if you can be part of giving that gift.
- When you open an envelope, ask God to give you insight and wisdom.
- When you flip a light switch, thank God for the power of the Holy Spirit.

And here's a bonus:

- When you pet a dog (or cat), thank God for his loyalty and love.

PAUSE TO PONDER

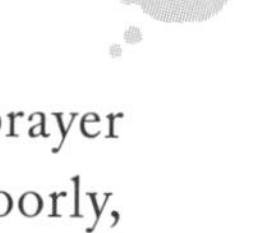

If you're like most believers, you consider prayer something you do. You might do it well or poorly, frequently or infrequently, but it's that Thing You Do When You Talk to God. Sometimes you're praying, and sometimes you're not praying.

The notion that you're *always* communicating with God might strike you as a bit…creepy.

Maybe there are times you'd rather God *not* be with you because you're pretty sure he wouldn't be favorably impressed with what you're saying or doing. So, for you, keeping prayer tightly segmented and predictable is actually something you prefer.

Unfortunately, it's not something God prefers.

He knows you, so your browser history won't surprise him. Ditto what you think when that attractive co-worker passes by. And your tax returns? Yup—he's already audited them.

So what do you have to lose by being transparent with God…and yourself?

Better yet, what do you have to gain?

Talk with God about how honest he thinks the two of you can be and still remain friends. You might discover something you haven't known before.

EXPERIMENT 1: Write It Out

You'll need a sidewalk or driveway (use yours), a rainless day (sorry, Seattle), and the ability to bend.

Write out a prayer for your neighborhood where your neighbors can see it. *That's* prayer that's outside the box.

Potentially awkward? Probably outside your comfort zone, but depending on what you write, both encouraging and supportive.

Ask God to bless the neighborhood, to keep your neighbors safe and secure. Ask for grace to be a good neighbor.

And write it in easily understood language, with words even the neighborhood kids can understand.

No medieval English. No weird, churchy words nobody understands.

Then don't wash off what you've written until it disappears on its own.

After this experiment, see what—if anything—changes regarding how your neighbors treat you. See what conversations are sparked.

After this experiment, talk with God about how this prayer did or didn't shift your views of prayer and how prayer fits into your life.

"The Lord is close to all who call on him, yes, to all who call on him in truth."

Psalm 145:18

PRAYER ADJUSTMENT: ASK JESUS WHAT YOU SHOULD PRAY ABOUT

Ever found yourself feeling a desire to pray but unsure what to say?

Here's a thought: Ask Jesus what to pray about. Perhaps there's something he has on the docket that you're not aware of.

Our friend Rick Lawrence says that sometimes he'll simply ask, "Jesus, what is it we need to talk about?" Then he'll be quiet and go with whatever pops into his head.

Rick sees that as part of having a childlike faith and maintaining an attachment to Jesus. He's depending on Jesus, not just for answers, but for questions as well.

Which just makes sense, when you think about it.

Jesus knows what's coming at you long before you see those challenges ride into view. He knows where you can be most helpful serving others. He's able to look past your distractions to what's really important.

So rather than wait until you've accumulated an agenda to discuss, just ask Jesus: What would *you* like to talk about?

Then wait.

And go with it.

See where it takes you.

PAUSE TO PONDER

When you give up the agenda in prayer, you're taking a risk. What if Jesus wants to dig into stuff you'd rather ignore? What if instead of working through your list of bless-mom-bless-dad-help-the-needy he wants to discuss your independent streak? Or that addiction you're good at hiding?

Giving Jesus control of the conversation is giving him permission to talk about what matters most.

Are you willing to do that?

Are you willing to go where he leads?

Jot or draw your sense of where a discussion like that might take you.

EXPERIMENT 1: Asking Jesus

Repeat after us: Jesus, what would you like to talk about?

Wait for something to pop into your mind.

Go with it.

See where the conversation takes you.

After trying this experiment, discuss with God: What did you think? Should we do this again? Why or why not?

"

Confess your
sins to each other
and pray for each other
so that you may be healed.
The earnest prayer of a
righteous person has
great power and
produces wonderful
results.

"

James 5:16

IF YOU'RE NOT SURE HOW THE HOLY SPIRIT FITS INTO PRAYER...

Here's the thing: You're not in this prayer thing alone.

Yes, God's friendship puts him squarely in the relationship. And there's Jesus, as well. But someone else is in the mix, too, and that's the Holy Spirit.

When Jesus was getting ready to return to heaven, his followers were understandably concerned. They'd lost him once already—temporarily—to the cross and tomb. And now he was sounding as if he was leaving again.

And not only that: He was saying it was *good* that he was leaving because someone else was coming to help in ways that would transform his followers.

It was a lot to take in, and even Jesus' closest disciples didn't really get the entire picture. Not at first. Not until they had an encounter with the Holy Spirit.

When Jesus was with his followers, they grew about as close as any friends could grow. They ate together, traveled together, hung out around the campfire together. They faced danger and disappointment together. His disciples heard Jesus teach and got a ringside seat as he performed miracles.

They got so close that Jesus told them they were no longer just his students or his servants—they were his friends.

But it was still an external relationship. There was still distance between them.

And then the Holy Spirit came—and the Spirit of God literally moved inside them. There was no longer any physical limitations separating those who love God from the God who loves them. Here's an astounding truth: God has set up shop in you.

We promised to not go all theological on you, so we won't. Suffice it to say that you have the same intimacy with God that the disciples experienced.

If you're a Christ-follower, you, too, have access to the same Spirit who showed up in a rush of wind and flickering of flame at Pentecost (Acts 2:1-4).

And that changes everything, prayer included.

One way it changes prayer is that, when you pray, the Holy Spirit is often softly guiding you. The Spirit is in every part of your friendship with God—not controlling it, not dictating how you feel about God, but guiding you toward spiritual wholeness and health. Which is to say, toward God.

And when there's turmoil in your life, when your thoughts are a swirl of want and need and you desperately need God but don't know how to reach out to him, that's where the Holy Spirit really shines.

Paul wrote this to the first-century church in Rome: "And the Holy Spirit helps us in our weakness. For example, we don't know what God wants us to pray for. But the Holy Spirit prays for us with groanings that cannot be expressed in words" (Romans 8:26).

How does the Holy Spirit fit into prayer? Everywhere, that's where.

And you're immeasurably richer for it.

PAUSE TO PONDER

Not every believer is comfortable with the Holy Spirit. Some Christian traditions focus a great deal on the Holy Spirit, and some don't.

How about you?

How does the idea that the Holy Spirit is in you and actively guiding you—including guiding you in prayer—sit with you?

Jesus saw the Spirit coming as a good thing. An essential thing. A wonderful thing.

In what ways are you comfortable with relying on the Spirit when you pray, and in what ways are you uncomfortable with it?

Jot your thoughts below.

If you've never thought much about the Holy Spirit, do this: Introduce yourself. If you're thankful for the help in drawing closer to God, say so.

IF YOU'RE FLAT-OUT TIRED OF PRAYING...

Hopefully the experiments you've tried as you've made your way through this little book have fanned your enthusiasm for prayer.

We know God's always eager to meet with you. Your coming to him again and again has given him ample opportunity to speak to you, to connect with you in fresh ways.

But if nothing is still happening for you, we have a solution.

Two, actually.

The first is this: Pray with others. Not necessarily with that small group from church where you all take turns going around a circle sharing "prayers and praises," which someone writes down so he can repeat them all back to God while the rest of you shut your eyes.

That's not real stuff. That's not going to do it for you.

Instead, call someone who knows Jesus and say, "I just can't pray. Can we get together to talk about that?"

Trust us—you'll hear a "yes."

When you meet, lay it all out. Share what you've tried, what seems to be between you and God, and why prayer feels like dragging a concrete block around with you. Be as honest as you can be and settle for nothing less from the person you're with.

Then listen. Perhaps God will answer your prayers about prayer through the person sitting across the café table from you. Perhaps what you need most is to invite someone else into your relationship with God, someone he can use to coach you.

And if it's not the first person you call, call someone else.

Keep seeking God however you can, and you'll find him. He promises.

And that second thing?

If you can't seem to stay awake while praying, then pray while standing up.

Seriously? You didn't think of that?

“

If you need wisdom,
ask our generous God, and
he will give it to you. He will
not rebuke you for asking.
But when you ask him, be sure
that your faith is in God alone.
Do not waver, for a person with
divided loyalty is as unsettled as
a wave of the sea that is blown
and tossed by the wind.
Such people should not
expect to receive anything
from the Lord.

”

James 1:5–7

PRAYER JOURNAL PAGES

Here's a short stack to get you started.

You have our permission to make as many copies as you'd like for your personal use, but please don't pass them around.

If you have friends or family who you think would find this experience useful, encourage them by buying them their own copy of this book. That way they'll have the entire experience—and they can make copies themselves.

Think of how much printer ink that'll save you.

And how it'll keep you from breaking a federal copyright law and everything.

Sort of a good idea all around, isn't it?

PRAYER JOURNAL

Part 1

Date: ______________

God, here's why I'd like to talk with you and how I feel right now…

Part 2

Date: ______________

Here's how I think you answered, God, and how I feel about your response...

Part 3

Date: ______________

God, let's talk about what happened. I'll tell you how I feel about you, and you tell me how you feel about me, okay?

PRAYER JOURNAL

Part 1

Date: ______________

God, here's why I'd like to talk with you and how I feel right now…

Part 2

Date: ______________

Here's how I think you answered, God, and how I feel about your response...

Part 3

Date: ____________

God, let's talk about what happened. I'll tell you how I feel about you, and you tell me how you feel about me, okay?

J.